DRESS and ADORNMENT

DRESS AND ADORNMENT

PHOTOGRAPHS BY PETER MAGUBANE

TEXT BY SANDRA KLOPPER

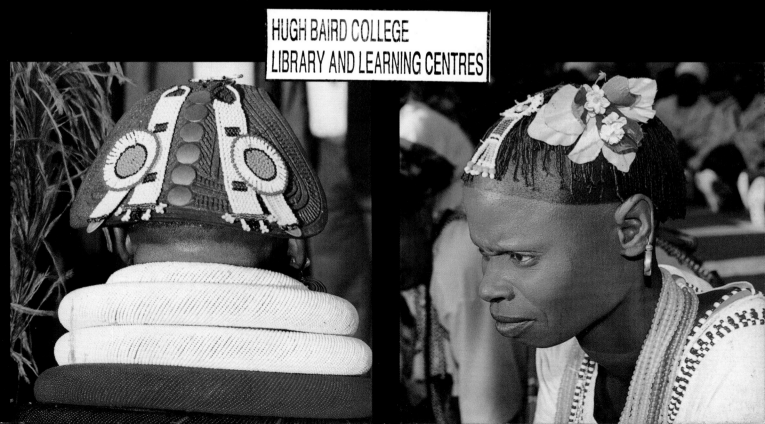

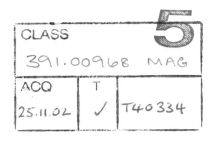
Published by Struik Publishers
(a division of New Holland Publishing (South Africa) (Pty) Ltd)

Cape Town • London • Sydney • Auckland

Garfield House
86 Edgware Road
W2 2EA London
United Kingdom

14 Aquatic Drive
Frenchs Forest
NSW 2086
Australia

80 McKenzie Street
Cape Town 8001
South Africa

218 Lake Road
Northcote, Auckland
New Zealand

Website: www.struik.co.za

ISBN 1 86872 514 6

Design director Janice Evans
Publishing manager Annlerie van Rooyen
Design Illana Fridkin
Managing editor Lesley Hay-Whitton
Proofreader Glynne Newlands
French translator Jean-Paul Houssière
German translator Friedel Herrmann

Reproduction by Hirt & Carter (Cape) Pty Ltd
Printed and bound by APP Printers, Singapore

Front cover: Bantwane novice diviners at their coming-out ceremony.
Back cover: Young Bantwane initiate.
Page 1: Married Ndebele woman.
Page 2 (left): Ndebele woman with neckrings.
Page 2 (right): Ndebele initiate wearing Middelburg blanket.
Page 3 (left): Bakôpa bride.
Page 3 (right): Characteristic Bantwane hairstyle.
Opposite: Young Tsonga initiates.
Page 6: Older Bakôpa married woman.

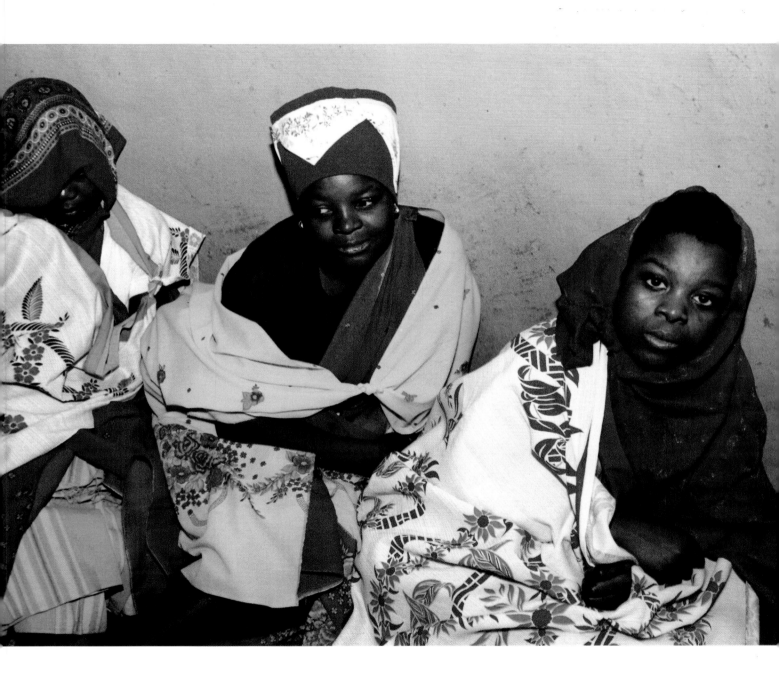

INTRODUCTION

Extravagant clothing and adornments are commonly adopted on special occasions such as weddings, the installation of chiefs, celebrations commemorating cultural and other heroes, the coming-out ceremonies of young women, and the joyous reception by friends and family members of pre- and post-pubescent male and female initiates following their return to their communities. This practice stems from a desire to give expression to particular social, political or religious values. In these situations certain forms of adornment, for instance beadwork, may be used to draw attention to a variety of social roles and identities. These include the age of the wearer, a woman's status as the mother of an initiate who has just undergone circumcision, or the ritual significance of certain colour combinations and designs.

In most cases specific kinds of dress and the use of various types of ornamentation are prescribed by traditions, but the clothing and adornment worn on special occasions also attest to the innovative use of materials like plastic beads, safety pins and other commercially manufactured objects and artefacts. Like the emergence of new styles of beadwork, the use of these materials highlights the fact that the traditional forms of dress and adornment produced by South Africa's rural communities have repeatedly been adapted to accommodate the changing circumstances and needs of contemporary traditionalists. More often than not, these forms of adornment nevertheless serve to underline conventional relations of authority and respect as well as deeply entrenched gender relations. This helps to explain why it is primarily women rather than men who continue to wear traditional forms of dress in most rural communities. In recent years, however, it has also become increasingly common for other South Africans, including former political exiles, to affirm a sense of pride in their rich cultural heritage by wearing the clothing and various forms of adornment associated with these communities.

The dress styles adopted by those seeking to show their respect for indigenous cultural traditions and practices often differ in important respects from those worn by rural traditionalists. This can be seen in the tendency to adopt hybrid styles of dress and adornment through the combination of various local forms with others borrowed from west and east African communities.

INTRODUCTION

En Afrique, comme ailleurs dans le monde, il est coutumier que des parures et costumes extravagants soient portés lors d'occasions spéciales comme les noces, les inaugurations de chefs, les cérémonies pour débutantes et les joyeuses festivités organisées par familles et amis, qui accueillent les jeunes garçons et filles au sein de leur communauté à la fin de leur période d'initiation. Cet usage provient du désir d'exprimer certaines valeurs sociales, politiques ou religieuses. Dans ces circonstances certaines formes d'ornements, faits de perles par exemple, sont portés afin d'affirmer une diversité d'identités et de conditions sociales. Celles-ci comprennent l'âge de l'individu, la position sociale de la mère d'un initié qui vient d'être circoncis, ou encore la signification rituelle de certaines combinaisons de couleurs ou de motifs.

Dans la plupart des cas, d'anciennes traditions imposent des costumes particuliers et le port de certaines parures, mais les costumes portés lors d'occasions spéciales témoignent aussi de l'usage novateur fait de produits de consommation modernes, comme les perles de plastique, les épingles de sûreté et autres objets manufacturés. Comme l'avènement de nouveaux styles dans la création d'objets perlés, l'utilisation de ces matériaux modernes montre que les communautés rurales de l'Afrique du Sud savent non seulement s'adapter aux circonstances changeantes, mais également satisfaire en même temps les exigences des traditionalistes contemporains. Le plus souvent ces genres d'ornements ont pour but de souligner non seulement les marques de respect traditionnelles, mais aussi les rapports bien établis entre hommes et femmes, ce qui explique pourquoi, dans la majorité des communautés rurales, ce sont plutôt celles-ci qui continuent à porter les vêtements traditionnels. Cependant, depuis quelques années, on découvre que de plus en plus de Sud-africains, y compris d'anciens exilés politiques, extériorisent la fierté qu'ils ont pour leur riche patrimoine culturel en portant les costumes et ornements traditionnels de ces communautés.

Toutefois, les styles diffèrent largement entre les costumes portés par ceux qui ne veulent que montrer leur respect pour la culture et les usages indigènes, et ceux portés par les traditionalistes ruraux. Ceci est visible dans la tendance aux costumes et ornements disparates et l'incorporation de styles d'Afrique occidentale et orientale.

EINFÜHRUNG

Ausgefallene Kleidung und schmückendes Zubehör wird zu besonderen Anlässen allgemein getragen, etwa bei Hochzeiten, Amtseinführung von Häuptlingen, Heldenfeiern, der festlichen Einführung junger Frauen in die Gesellschaft und dem freudigen Empfang, den Familie und Freunde männlichen und weiblichen Initianden bereiten, die nach Absolvierung der Initiationsschule heimkehren. Dieser Brauch erwächst aus dem Bedürfnis, besonderen gesellschaftlichen, politischen oder religiösen Werten Ausdruck zu verleihen. Bei solchen Anlässen dienen Schmuck und Ergänzungen – etwa aus Perlen – dazu, die Aufmerksamkeit auf diverse gesellschaftliche Stellungen und Merkmale zu lenken. Hierzu zählt das Alter des Trägers/der Trägerin, der Status einer Frau, deren Sohn gerade die Beschneidung durchgemacht hat, und die rituelle Bedeutung bestimmter Farbkombinationen oder Muster.

In den meisten Fällen sind Kleidung und verschiedenartiger Schmuck laut Überlieferungen vorgeschrieben, dennoch zeugen gerade Kleidung und Schmuck zu besonderen Anlässen auch von innovativem Gebrauch von Plastikperlen, Sicherheitsnadeln und anderen kommerziell erzeugten Artikeln. Genau wie die Entwicklung neuer Perlenmuster, unterstreicht auch die Nutzung dieser Gebrauchsgüter die Tatsache, daß traditionelle Kleidung und Schmuckartikel der ländlichen Volksgruppen in Südafrika wiederholte Anpassungen erfahren haben, um den veränderten Umständen und dem derzeitigen Traditionsgefühl Rechnung zu tragen. Dennoch unterstreichen diese schmückenden Ergänzungen mehrheitlich das konventionelle Verhältnis von Autorität und Respekt, sowie eine tief verwurzelte Beziehung der Geschlechter. Daher sind es zumeist die Frauen, die in ländlichen Gebieten weiterhin traditionelle Kleidung tragen. In jüngster Zeit kommt es jedoch häufiger vor, daß auch andere Südafrikaner, einschließlich ehemaliger politischer Verbannter, ihren Stolz auf ihr reiches Kulturerbe betonen, indem sie Kleidung und Schmuck einheimischer Volksgruppen anlegen.

Aber der Kleidungsstil, der aus einem Bedürfnis heraus getragen wird, dem kulturellen Brauchtum Anerkennung zu zollen, unterscheidet sich oft in wesentlichen Punkten von dem der echten Traditionalisten. Dies tritt deutlich in der Neigung zutage, Kleidungsstücke und Schmuck von verschiedenen Völkern miteinander oder mit solchen aus West- und Ostafrika zu verbinden.

The beadwork worn by young Zulu women at the annual Reed Ceremony held at one of King Zwelethini's royal homesteads in northern KwaZulu-Natal attests to regional variations in style. These differences are reflected in the use of bead colours and patterns.

Les ornements perlés portés par les jeunes zouloues pour la cérémonie annuelle des roseaux (Reed Ceremony), dans le Nord du KwaZulu-Natal, démontrent la diversité des styles régionaux. Les différences dans l'usage des couleurs et des motifs sont évidentes.

Der Perlenschmuck, den junge Zulufrauen zur jährlichen ‚Schilfzeremonie' tragen, wie sie im nördlichen KwaZulu-Natal abgehalten wird, weist regionale Stilvariationen auf. Die Unterschiede zeigen sich in den Farben und Mustern der Perlenarbeiten.

While some beadwork styles still rely on small glass beads, others use larger plastic beads that have recently become readily available. The items worn by initiates often combine small and large beads in innovative ways.

Alors que certains styles d'ornements exigent encore des petites perles de verre, d'autres utilisent les nouvelles perles de plastique, plus grosses. Les ornements consistent d'une combinaison de styles anciens et modernes.

Einige Perlenarbeiten sind noch aus kleinen Glasperlen angefertigt, andere enthalten größere Plastikperlen, die jetzt allgemein verfügbar sind. Die von Initianden getragenen Artikel verbinden beide auf innovative Art und Weise.

The beadwork worn by South Sotho initiates on their return to the community is generally given to them by their mothers. Although today it is less common to find women who practise this art form, many still make the beadwork items worn by their sons.

Les ornements perlés portés par les initiés south sothos sont offerts par leur mère. De moins en moins de femmes pratiquent cette forme d'art, mais nombreuses sont celles qui fabriquent encore les ornements portés par leur fils.

Den Perlenschmuck, den Initianden der Süd-Sotho anläßlich ihrer Heimkehr in die Gemeinschaft anlegen, haben sie gewöhnlich von ihren Müttern erhalten. Weniger Frauen üben heute diese Kunst aus, aber für ihre Söhne fertigen noch viele Perlenarbeiten an.

Most South Sotho women wear richly decorated grass masks during their initiation into adult status. Although these masks are still adorned in a wide variety of beadwork patterns and colours, many modern examples are covered in brightly coloured tufts of wool. This can be ascribed to the fact that young women seldom choose to learn the complex art of beadwork today.

La majorité des femmes south sothos portent des masques d'herbes richement décorés avec des perles pendant leur période d'initiation. On trouve également de nombreux exemplaires couverts de touffes de laine. La raison en est que les jeunes femmes d'aujourd'hui n'apprennent plus que rarement l'art complexe de décorer avec des perles.

Die meisten Frauen der Süd-Sotho tragen anläßlich ihrer Einführung ins Erwachsenenleben reich verzierte Grasmasken. Obwohl diese Masken noch immer bunte Perlenmuster aufweisen, sind die neuzeitlichen oft mit farbenfreudigen Wollbüscheln bedeckt. Das ist darauf zurückzuführen, daß junge Frauen sich heutzutage selten darum bemühen, die komplizierte Kunst der Perlenarbeit zu erlernen.

In contemporary KwaZulu-Natal, married Zulu women commonly wear large beaded capes as a sign of respect to both the ancestors and their husbands' families. These capes, which vary significantly in style from one region to another, are worn in combination with leather skirts made from the hides of ritually slaughtered animals. In many cases, these heavy, pleated skirts are worn under embroidered cloths or beaded aprons.

Dans le KwaZulu-Natal d'aujourd'hui, les femmes mariées portent habituellement de grandes capes perlées en signe de respect pour leur belle-famille et les ancêtres. Ces capes, dont le style varie sensiblement d'une région à l'autre, sont portées avec des jupons en cuir, venant de la peau d'animaux sacrifiés. Dans de nombreux cas, ces lourds jupons plissés sont couverts de tissus brodés ou perlés.

Im heutigen KwaZulu-Natal tragen verheiratete Frauen vielfach große, mit Perlen bestickte Umhänge als Zeichen der Achtung gegenüber Ahnen und Schwiegerfamilie. Diese Umhänge, die stilistisch große regionale Unterschiede aufweisen, werden zusammen mit einem Rock, der aus den Fellen rituell geschlachteter Tiere angefertigt wird, getragen. Häufig werden über diesem schweren Faltenrock noch bestickte Tücher oder Perlenschurze getragen.

Ndebele mothers also wear ornately beaded capes and aprons on ritual occasions. These items are worn in combination with bulbous beaded and brass leg rings. In the past, such rings were attached permanently to the legs, arms and necks of newly married women.

Les mères ndebeles elles aussi, portent des capes et des tabliers ornementés de perles lors des occasions rituelles. Avec ces costumes, elles portent aux jambes des gros anneaux de perles et de cuivre. Autrefois, ces anneaux étaient attachés en permanence.

Ndebelemütter tragen auch perlenbestickte Umhänge und Schurze zu rituellen Anlässen. Dazu kommen dicke Beinreife aus Perlen und Messingringe. Früher wurden solche Metall-ringe am Hals und an den Armen und Beinen von vermählten Frauen ständig getragen.

The neck rings traditionally worn by married Bantwane (*left*) and Ndebele women varied considerably in size and shape. Although none of the neck rings worn today by Bantwane women are characterized by distinctive beadwork patterns, they are made in a variety of colours. Aesthetic rather than symbolic concerns appear to be the reason why women wear rings covered in white beads against the face.

Les colliers traditionnels portés par les femmes mariées bantwanes (*à gauche*) et ndebeles varient sensiblement en style et contour. Bien que les colliers portés de nos jours par les Bantwanes ne soient caractérisés par aucun style en particulier, ils sont fabriqués dans de nombreuses couleurs. Les colliers de perles blanches portés contre le visage ne le sont que pour raison esthétique plutôt que symbolique.

Die Halsringe, die traditionell von verheirateten Frauen der Bantwane (*links*) und Ndebele getragen wurden, wiesen deutliche Unterschiede in Größe und Form auf. Obgleich heutzutage keine dieser Halsringe der Bantwanefrauen irgendwelche typischen Perlenmuster aufweisen, gibt es sie in einer Vielzahl von Farben. Es hat aber wohl mehr ästhetische Gründe, daß die Frauen die weißen Perlenreife in Gesichtsnähe getragen

Beaded body rings are often combined with other beadwork items like the long trains worn by married Ndebele women. By wearing beaded and embroidered panels over their hips at coming-out ceremonies, unmarried women draw attention to their sexuality.

Les ceintures perlées sont souvent combinées avec d'autres ornements, comme les traînes des mariées ndebeles. Lors des cérémonies d'initiation, les femmes célibataires portent sur les hanches des plis brodés pour attirer l'attention sur leur sexualité.

Leibringe werden oft mit anderen Perlenarbeiten kombiniert, wie den langen Schleppen verheirateter Ndebelefrauen. Indem sie bei ihrer Einführung perlenverzierte Hüftschurze tragen, lenken unverheiratete Frauen die Aufmerksamkeit auf ihre Sexualität.

On certain ceremonial occasions young Bantwane women wear several beaded body rings around their waists and on their upper arms. These rings are always worn with fringed skirts, decorated beadwork panels and long bifurcated leather back aprons.

A l'occasion de certaines célébrations, les jeunes femmes bantwanes portent plusieurs anneaux perlés autour de la taille et aux bras. Ces anneaux sont portés avec des jupes frangées ornées de perles, et à l'arrière un long tablier de cuir divisé en deux.

Zu gewissen zeremoniellen Anlässen tragen junge Bantwanefrauen mehrere Perlenreife um Körper und Oberarme. Diese Ringe werden immer zusammen mit Fransenröckchen, Perlenschmuck und langen, gespalteten Lederschurzen über der Hinterpartie getragen.

Young Zulu women in the lower Drakensberg region wear long strings of beads attached to studded waistbands. Inspired by beadwork associated with Xhosa-speaking communities further south, these beaded strings create spectacular effects during dance sequences.

Dans la région du bas Drakensberg, les jeunes zouloues portent des ceintures cloutées où sont attachés de longs colliers de perles. Inspirés de leurs voisins du sud, les Xhosas, ces colliers produisent des effets spectaculaires dans les mouvements de danse.

In den unteren Regionen der Drakensberge tragen junge Zulufrauen lange Perlenschnüre an nietenverzierten Hüftgürteln. Dies geht auf den Einfluß der weiter südlich lebenden Xhosagruppen zurück. Die Perlenschnüre erzeugen beim Tanzen einen tollen Effekt.

Rural traditionalists frequently add letters and words to their beadwork garments. There are various reasons for this, but it may convey affection in the case of mothers of South Sotho initiates. Since the African National Congress came to power in 1994 it has become common for people to declare their support for this organization through beadwork.

Les traditionalistes incluent souvent des mots et des lettres dans les motifs de leurs costumes. Dans le cas des initiés south sothos, c'est une façon pour les mères de démontrer leur affection. Depuis l'accession au pouvoir de l'ANC en 1994, il est fréquent pour les gens de montrer leur appui pour l'organisation, en incorporant des motifs appropriés dans leurs ouvrages.

Auch Buchstaben und Wörter werden oftmals in Kleidungsstücke aus Perlen eingearbeitet. Hierfür gibt es unterschiedliche Gründe. Im Falle der Süd-Sotho-Initianden drückt es Mutterliebe aus. Seit der Afrikanische Nationalkongreß 1994 an die Macht kam, wird Unterstützung für die Organisation auch durch Perlenarbeit bekundet.

Bantwane women sometimes weave words into the beaded panels worn at initiation and other ceremonies. These words usually indicate the region or village from which the wearer hails, but these beadwork panels are also decorated with individual letters and abstract patterns not intended to communicate a message or meaning.

Les femmes bantwanes incorporent parfois des mots dans les motifs de perles qu'elles portent aux initiations et autres cérémonies. Souvent ces mots indiquent la région ou le village d'origine de la personne, mais ces ornements comprennent aussi des lettres et motifs abstraits qui n'ont pas de sens précis.

Die Frauen der Bantwane weben mitunter Wörter in die Perlenbänder, die bei Initiationsfeiern und anderen Zeremonien getragen werden. Oft zeigen diese Wörter an, aus welchem Bezirk oder Dorf die Trägerin stammt, aber die Perlenbänder enthalten auch Buchstaben und abstrakte Motive, die keine besondere Bedeutung haben.

In most South African communities, ritual specialists usually wear a variety of garments made of red, white and black beads. These three colours are commonly associated with the ancestors who communicate their needs to the living through ritual specialists.

Dans la plupart des communautés, les spécialistes rituels portent plusieurs vêtements fait de perles rouges, blanches et noires. Ces trois couleurs sont liées aux ancêtres qui communiquent leurs désirs aux vivants par l'intermédiaire de ces spécialistes.

Bei den meisten Volksgruppen Südafrikas tragen die Ritualisten verschiedene Bekleidungsstücke aus roten, weißen und schwarzen Perlen. Diese drei Farben werden mit den Ahnen in Verbindung gebracht, die ihre Forderungen durch diese Personen kundtun.

Although the wearing of wild animal skins has become rare, dignitaries like Zulu king Zwelethini, Chief Mangosuthu Buthelezi and Prince Gideon Zulu (*opposite, right to left*) still appear in leopard skin garments on special occasions. The practice of making garments from the leather of domesticated animals, notably goats and cattle, is however still comparatively widespread.

Le port de peaux d'animaux sauvages est devenu rare, mais des dignitaires comme le roi zoulou Zwelethini, son oncle le prince Gideon Zulu, et le chef Mangosuthu Buthelezi, se montrent de temps en temps en peau de léopard lors d'occasions spéciales. L'utilisation de cuir d'animaux domestiques, notamment de chèvres et de bovins, pour la manufacture de vêtements, est toujours répandue.

Das Tragen von Fellen wilder Tiere ist selten geworden, aber hochstehende Persönlichkeiten, wie der Zulukönig Zwelethini, sein Onkel, Prinz Gideon Zulu, und Häuptling Mangosuthu Buthelezi treten noch immer bei besonderen Anlässen in Leopardenfellen auf. Die Felle von Ziegen und Rindern werden jedoch weiterhin relativ häufig zu Bekleidungsstücken verarbeitet.

Since leopard skins are both rare and expensive, those who wish to signify their social or ritual status by wearing skins of this kind tend to make garments from cotton cloth printed with leopard markings. People also mark antelope skins with leopard-like spots.

Comme les peaux de léopard sont rares et très chères, ceux qui désirent afficher leur position sociale en portant de tels costumes, les fabriquent en imitation de coton imprimé. Les gens marquent aussi des peaux d'antilopes avec des taches de léopard.

Da Leopardenfelle rar und teuer sind, verwenden jene, die ihre gesellschaftliche Stellung durch das Tragen solcher Felle hervorheben möchten, mit Leopardenmuster bedruckte Baumwollstoffe. Auch Antilopenfelle werden mit ‚Leopardentupfen' versehen.

At church services and on other ritual occasions, South Sotho women wear colourful dresses decorated with strips of bright braid. Like the dresses worn by Herero women in Namibia, these garments were inspired by the clothing of 19th century missionary families.

Les femmes south sothos portent des robes ornées de galons aux couleurs vives pour les offices religieux et autres occasions rituelles. Comme les robes des femmes Hereros en Namibie, ces vêtements sont inspirés par l'habillement des missionnaires du 19ième.

Zum Kirchgang und bei anderen rituellen Anlässen tragen die Frauen der Süd-Sotho farbenfreudige, bortenverzierte Kleider. Genau wie die Tracht der Herero in Namibia wurde diese Kleidung durch die der Missionarsfrauen im 19. Jahrhundert angeregt.

In common with the influence of missionaries elsewhere in South Africa, the flowing cotton garments and elaborate scarves adopted by Xhosa-speaking women in the 19th century are based on hats and dresses worn by Victorian women. This clothing replaced the simpler, much shorter garments made from the leather of goats and cattle.

Le style des vêtements de coton et des foulards que portent les femmes xhosas remonte au 19ième. Il est basé sur l'habille-ment des missionnaires de l'époque, dont l'influence était étendue en Afrique du Sud. Ces costumes remplaçaient ceux plus simples, et plus courts, fait en peau de chèvre et de vache.

So, wie sich der Einfluß der Missio-nare auch anderswo in Südafrika bemerkbar gemacht hat, leiten sich Baumwollkleider und Kopf-tücher, die bei den Xhosa-Frauen im 19. Jahrhundert eingeführt wur-den, von viktorianischer Frauen-kleidung her und ersetzten die ein-facheren und kürzeren Kleidungs-stücke aus Rinds- oder Ziegenleder.

Cotton and other cloths produced for the rural market are commonly worn by ritual specialists and other traditionalists. Various cloths are often juxtaposed to create striking or symbolic combinations. Ritual specialists also use accessories like fly whisks, beaded headdresses and leather aprons to underline their capacity to mediate with the ancestors.

Les étoffes fabriquées pour la clientèle rurale sont fréquemment portées par les spécialistes rituels et les traditionalistes. Souvent, plusieurs pièces sont accolées pour des raisons symboliques. Les spécialistes rituels utilisent aussi des chasse-mouches, des bandeaux de perles et des tabliers de cuir pour afficher leur aptitude de communiquer avec les ancêtres.

Ritualisten verwenden Baumwolle und andere Stoffe, die für den ländlichen Absatzmarkt erzeugt werden. Symbolische oder außergewöhnliche Kombinationen werden durch die Verbindung verschiedener Stoffarten erzielt. Um ihre Fähigkeit in der Ahnenunterhandlung hervorzuheben, tragen sie Fliegenwedel, Lederschurze und Perlen im Haar.

Ritual specialists wear commercially produced cloths printed in red, white and black to draw attention to their status. In contrast to the symbolic significance attached to these colours, the patterns on the cloths generally have a purely decorative function.

Les spécialistes rituels portent des étoffes imprimées en rouge, blanc et noir, pour attirer l'attention sur leur position. Alors que les couleurs ont un sens symbolique, les motifs ornant le tissu n'ont qu'une simple fonction décorative.

Rot, Weiß und Schwarz haben symbolische Bedeutung, und Ritualisten tragen fabrik-mäßig hergestellte Stoffe in diesen Farben, um auf ihre gesellschaftliche Stellung aufmerksam zu machen. Die Stoffmuster dagegen sind nur ein dekoratives Attribut.

The cloths worn by rural traditionalists vary considerably from one area to another. While the Swazi sometimes wear cloths commemorating the lives of important leaders, Venda cloths are characterized by colourful stripes interspersed with bold black lines.

Les étoffes portées par les traditionalistes varient fortement d'une région à l'autre. Alors que celles des Swazis commémorent la vie de chefs important, celles des Vendas sont typiques par leurs bandes de couleurs entrecoupées de larges lignes noires.

Traditionalisten der verschiedenen Regionen tragen unterschiedlich bedruckte Stoffe. Wo die Swasi mitunter bedeutende Führer auf ihren Stoffen zur Schau tragen, kennzeichnet sich die Kleidung der Venda durch farbenfreudige Streifen und breite schwarze Striche.

Most traditional communities wear
distinctively coloured blankets
on ritual and other occasions.
Among certain Ndebele groups,
for example, male initiates adopt
red, yellow and blue 'Middelburg'
blankets, named after one of
the largest towns in the area
historically occupied by present-
day Ndebele communities.

La plupart des communautés traditionnelles porte des couvertures
avec des couleurs spéciales lors
des occasions rituelles et autres.
Parmi certains groupes ndebeles,
par exemple, les initiés ont adopté
des couvertures rouges, jaunes et
bleues 'Middelburg', appelées ainsi
d'après un des plus grands centres
de la région, habité par la communauté ndebele d'aujourd'hui.

Die meisten Volksgruppen tragen
Decken in besonderen Farben zu
rituellen Anlässen und anderen
Gelegenheiten. Männliche Initianden der Ndebele, etwa, nehmen
rot-gelb-blaue ‚Middelburg'-
Decken, benannt nach einer der
größten Städte im ursprünglichen
Heimatgebiet der heute verstreut
lebenden Ndebelegruppen.

On their return to the community, Tswana initiates wear blankets characterized by abstract patterns against a background of detailed motifs. Initiates in the cold mountains of Lesotho (*opposite, right*) wrap themselves in blankets made for this market.

Pour leur retour au sein de la communauté, les initiés tswanas portent des couvertures aux sujets abstraits sur un fond très fouillé. Dans les montagnes froides du Lesotho, les initiés s'emmitouflent dans des couvertures fabriquées spécialement pour ce marché.

Zur Rückkehr in die Gemeinschaft tragen Initianden der Tswana Decken mit abstrakten Motiven auf einem kleingemusterten Hintergrund. In der kalten Bergluft von Lesotho wickeln sich die Initianden in Decken, die eigens für diesen Markt hergestellt werden.

Among the Bantwane, women of all ages shave part of their heads and dress their hair with oil and other substances on important ritual occasions. In some cases, women wear wigs made from blackened, string-like materials, obviating the need to shave the head.

Parmi les Bantwanes, les femmes de tout âge se rasent le crâne et s'enduisent les cheveux d'huile et autres substances à l'occasion d'importants événements rituels. Dans certains cas, elles portent des perruques faites de cordelettes noircies.

Zu wichtigen rituellen Anlässen rasieren sich Bantwane-Frauen aller Altersgruppen den Kopf und reiben das Haar unter anderem mit Öl ein. Mitunter tragen sie auch Perücken aus schwarzen Schnüren, weil sie sich dann die Kopfrasur ersparen.

On special occasions, Bantwane and Bakôpa girls and women decorate their heads with beautifully beaded ornaments, feathers, commercially produced everlasting flowers and old coins. By drawing attention to the women, these decorations highlight important aspects of their femininity, and therefore also their identities as mothers and daughters.

Pour les occasions spéciales, les femmes bantwanes et bakôpas parent leurs cheveux de magnifiques ornements perlés, avec des plumes, des fleurs artificielles et des pièces de monnaie. Tout en attirant l'attention sur les femmes, ces ornements soulignent aussi d'importants aspects de leur féminité, et par conséquent de leur identité de mères et de filles.

Zu festlichen Anlässen schmücken Mädchen und Frauen der Bantwane und Bakôpa ihre Köpfe mit hübschen Perlenornamenten, Federn, künst-lichen Blumen und alten Münzen. Da diese Verzierungen die Aufmerksamkeit auf die Trägerin lenken, dient der Schmuck letztendlich der Betonung wichtiger Aspekte ihrer Weiblichkeit und somit auch ihrer gesellschaftlichen Stellung als Mütter und Töchter.

Bantwane brides and older women shave their heads and wear detachable headdresses similar to the hairstyles of female initiates passing through puberty. These elaborately decorated headdresses underline the women's importance as potential or actual mothers.

Les jeunes mariées et femmes bantwanes adultes se rasent le crâne et portent des coiffes semblables à la coiffure des initiées d'âge pubère. Ces coiffes très ornementées soulignent l'importance de ces femmes, soit comme mères actuelles, soit comme mères en puissance.

Bräute und ältere Frauen der Bantwane rasieren sich den Kopf und tragen losen Kopfschmuck, der den Frisuren der Initiandinnen bei den Pubertätsriten ähnelt. Dieser kunstvoll verzierte Kopfschmuck unterstreicht die Bedeutung der Frauen als Mütter oder potentielle Mütter.

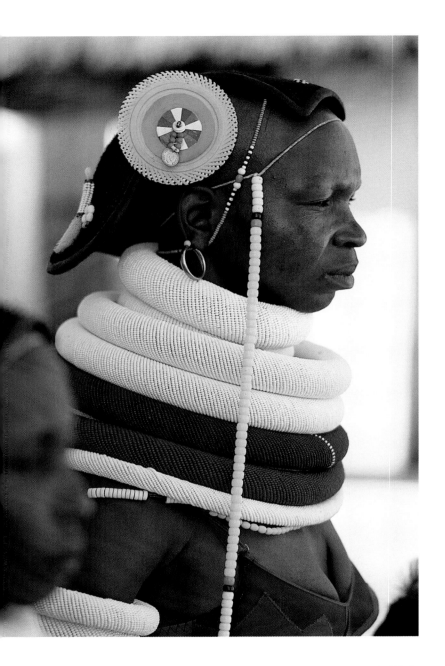

On ritual occasions married women from rural areas often wear elaborate headdresses. They are now generally detachable, but in the past women usually affirmed their marital status through the adoption of permanent headdresses fashioned in part from their hair. The headdresses of women from KwaZulu-Natal usually flare upwards from a colourful decorated headband signifying their respect for their husbands and parents-in-law.

A l'occasion d'événements rituels, les femmes mariées de la campagne portent souvent des coiffes complexes. De nos jours elles sont détachables, mais dans le passé les femmes indiquaient leur position d'épouse en portant en permanence une coiffe faite partiellement avec leurs cheveux. Les coiffes des femmes du KwaZulu-Natal s'évasent normalement vers le haut au départ d'un bandeau orné, symbolique de la déférence d'une épouse envers sa belle-famille et son mari.

Zu rituellen Anlässen tragen Frauen in ländlichen Gebieten oft reich verzierten Kopfschmuck. Heutzutage ist er meist abnehmbar, aber in der Vergangenheit zeigten Frauen ihren Ehestand durch teilweise aus eignem Haar geschaffenen, festen Kopfschmuck an. Frauen im heutigen KwaZulu-Natal tragen oft den Kopfschmuck hinter einem farbenfreudig dekorierten Stirnband, womit sie Achtung vor dem Ehemann und den Schwiegereltern bezeugen.

Headdresses worn by Zulu women from KwaZulu-Natal's Tugela Ferry region (*above, left*) differ markedly from those found in the Valley of a Thousand Hills near Durban (*opposite*). In some cases, colour and other decorative embellishments are used to signify the woman's support for prominent politicians like Chief Mangosuthu Buthelezi (*above, right*).

Les coiffes des zouloues mariées de la région de Tugela Ferry (*ci-dessus, à gauche*) diffèrent sensiblement de celles de la Vallée des mille collines (*ci-contre*), près de Durban. Dans certains cas, les femmes portent des ornements spéciaux pour marquer leur appui pour d'importants politiciens, tel que le chef Mangosuthu Buthelezi (*ci-dessus, à droite*).

Der Kopfschmuck der Zulu-Frauen in dem Landstrich bei Tugela Ferry (*oben, links*) unterscheidet sich deutlich von dem der Frauen im Tal der Tausend Hügel (*gegenüber*) bei Durban. In manchen Fällen deuten Farben und andere dekorative Elemente auf die Unterstützung der Trägerin für Häuptling Mangosuthu Buthelezi (*oben, rechts*).

The headdresses worn by women of the *Ibandla lamaNazaretha* (independent Shembe church) are usually covered in bands of beadwork. Betrothed women who are about to leave home cover their heads with hairnets and commercially manufactured hairpins.

Les coiffes des femmes de *Ibandla lamaNazaretha* (secte indépendante Shembe) sont normalement couvertes de bandes perlées. Les fiancées qui vont bientôt quitter leur famille, se couvrent les cheveux avec un filet et des épingles à cheveux.

Die Kopfbedeckung der Frauen der *Ibandla lamaNazaretha* (unabhängige Shembe-Kirche) ist meist mit Perlenbändern verkleidet. Verlobte Frauen, die bald das Elternhaus verlassen, bedecken ihr Haar mit handelsüblichen Haarnetzen und Haarnadeln.

Although many women no longer wear traditional headdresses, they still tend to show respect for their husbands and parents-in-law by covering their heads with scarves. On special occasions, these scarves are often shaped into elaborate styles.

Bien que de nombreuses femmes ne portent plus les coiffes traditionnelles, elles démontrent toujours leur respect pour leur mari et sa famille en se couvrant la tête de foulards. Pour les occasions spéciales, ces foulards sont souvent confectionnés dans des styles compliqués.

Obwohl viele Frauen nicht mehr die traditionellen Kopfbedeckungen tragen, bedecken sie doch den Kopf mit einem Schal, um Ehemann und Schwiegereltern Achtung zu zollen. Zu besonderen Anlässen werden diese Schals zu kunstvollen Turbanen verschlungen.

Both Xhosa (*left*) and South Sotho (*opposite*) women sometimes fashion their head scarves to form hat-like structures. Considerable skill is needed to form these ornate styles, which are generally chosen with a view to complementing the colour or design of their dresses and other important accessories like beadwork.

Les femmes xhosas (*à gauche*) et south sothos (*ci-contre*) donnent parfois à leurs foulards la forme d'un chapeau. Il faut un talent considérable pour façonner ces styles compliqués. Le but de ceux-ci est de complémenter la couleur ou les motifs du costume, ainsi que d'autres accessoires importants, comme les ornements perlés.

Sowohl die Frauen der Xhosa (*links*), als auch die der Süd-Sotho (*gegenüber*) falten ihre Kopftücher mitunter in hutartige Formen. Diese kunstvollen Gebilde zu bewerkstelligen, erfordert erhebliches Geschick. Der Stil wird im allgemeinen gewählt, um Farbe und Schnitt des Kleides oder andere wichtige Ergänzungen, wie etwa den Perlenschmuck, zu unterstreichen.

Head scarves worn by Xhosa women from the Eastern Cape are generally decorated with carefully spaced parallel lines stitched in white cotton against a dark blue, green or brown background. Produced with the aid of hand-operated sewing machines, these scarves are increasingly commonly sold as table cloths and wall hangings in curio shops located in major urban centres such as Cape Town.

Les femmes xhosas de l'Eastern Cape décorent souvent leurs foulards en cousant minutieusement des bandes de coton blanc sur un fond bleu, vert ou brun foncé. Confectionnés à l'aide d'anciennes machines à coudre, ces foulards sont fréquemment vendus comme nappes ou tapisseries dans les magasins de souvenirs des grands centres urbains, comme à Cape Town.

Xhosafrauen am Ostkap schmücken ihre Kopftücher meistens mit sorgfältig auseinander plazierten Stickreihen in Weiß gegen einen blauen, grünen oder braunen Hintergrund. Diese Kopftücher werden mit Hilfe handbetriebener Näh-maschinen angefertigt und in städtischen Gebieten wie Kapstadt werden sie zuneh-mend in Andenkenläden als Tischtücher und Wandbehänge verkauft.

Ndebele women generally decorate their heads with beaded bands. Like the bands worn by male initiates on their return to the community, these may be decorated with old coins. Only some beadwork is used to highlight the gender or the age of the wearer.

Les femmes ndebeles parent généralement leur tête avec des bandeaux. Comme ceux des initiés qui retournent dans leur communauté, ces bandeaux peuvent être ornés de vieilles pièces de monnaie. Une partie des perles indique le sexe ou l'âge du porteur.

Ndebelefrauen schmücken ihre Köpfe gewöhnlich mit Perlenbändern. Genau wie die Bänder männlicher Initianden bei der Heimkehr, sind diese teils mit alten Münzen verziert. Nur gewisser Perlenschmuck zeigt Alter und Geschlecht der Trägerin an.

A few married Ndebele women still have brass rings permanently attached to their necks (*left*). But, because most women no longer wear traditional forms of dress on a daily basis, these rings now have clasps (*opposite*), thereby allowing women to reserve them for special occasions like weddings.

Peu de femmes mariées ndebeles portent encore des anneaux de cuivre autour du cou en permanence (*à gauche*). Cependant, puisque la majorité ne portent plus les costumes traditionnels quotidiennement, ces anneaux sont maintenant pourvus d'un fermoir (*ci-contre*), permettant de ne les mettre que pour des occasions spéciales, comme les noces.

Einige wenige Ndebelefrauen tragen noch die permanent um den Hals befestigten Messingringe (*links*). Aber da die meisten Frauen nicht mehr im Alltag in Volkstracht herumgehen, haben diese Ringe jetzt Verschlüsse (*gegenüber*), damit die Frauen sie nur zu besonderen Anlässen wie Hochzeiten anlegen können.

Unlike the headdresses worn by married women, the styles of male headdresses tend to be dictated as much by personal choice as by convention. The probable reason for this is that men seldom use headdresses to underline their marital status.

Le style des coiffes d'hommes, contrairement à celui des coiffes des femmes mariées, a tendance à être inspiré plus par choix personnel que par tradition. La raison probable est que les hommes portent rarement une coiffe pour indiquer leur situation conjugale.

Im Gegensatz zu dem Kopfschmuck der verheirateten Frauen ist die Kopfbedeckung der Männer ebenso vom persönlichen Geschmack wie vom Brauchtum beeinflußt. Der Grund dafür ist wohl, daß Männer selten durch Kopfbedeckung auf ihren Ehestand hinweisen.

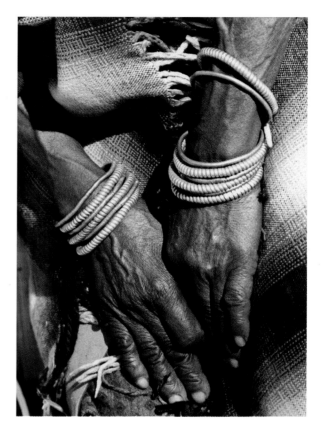

In the past metal bangles made from imported brass and copper wire were traded for indigenous furs and ivory. Men often bought their wives large numbers of these bangles, which symbolized wealth and status. Today bangles are made from cheaper tin alloys.

Dans le passé, des bracelets de fil de cuivre et de laiton importé, étaient troqués contre des fourrures et de l'ivoire indigènes. Les hommes achetaient souvent de ces bracelets en grands nombres pour leurs femmes, indiquant ainsi leur fortune et position sociale.

Früher wurden Ringe aus importiertem Messing und Kupfer gegen einheimische Pelze und Elfenbein gehandelt. Männer kauften ihren Frauen diese Reife, die Wohlstand und Rang symbolisierten. Heute werden sie aus billigeren Zinnlegierungen hergestellt.

Bantwane (*opposite*) and Pedi (*right*) initiates discard everyday clothing before entering the initiation lodge. The adoption of grass garments and ornaments alludes to fertility, and hence to their future roles as wives and mothers. During their confinement in these initiation lodges, girls receive instruction in appropriate social and sexual behaviour.

Les initiées bantwanes (*ci-contre*) et pedis (*à droite*) se débarrassent de leurs habits ordinaires avant d'entrer à l'école d'initiation. Le nouveau costume orné d'herbes qu'elles portent désormais, évoque la fécondité, donc leurs futurs rôles d'épouses et de mères. Durant leur réclusion à l'école d'initiation, elles sont instruites en matières sociales et sexuelles.

Ehe sie die Behausungen betreten, wo der Einführungskurs abgehalten wird, legen die Initianden der Bantwane (*gegenüber*) und Pedi (*rechts*) ihre Alltagsgewänder ab. Die Bekleidung aus Gras weist auf Fruchtbarkeit hin und damit auch auf ihre zukünftigen Rollen als Frauen und Mütter. Während ihrer Absonderung in diesen Initiationslagern werden die Mädchen in angemessenem Verhalten im Sexualbereich und Gemeinschaftsleben unterrichtet.

When male and female initiates return to the community following their seclusion in initiation lodges, they are often given sweets and gifts like jewellery and watches, which symbolize their success in surviving the hardships encountered during this period of transition. Initiates take great pride in displaying these objects, which are usually given to them by their mothers or other members of their families.

Quand les initiés, garçons et filles, retournent dans leur communauté suivant leur période de réclusion dans les écoles d'initiation, ils reçoivent souvent des douceurs et autres présents, tels que des montres ou des bijoux. Ceci symbolise leur réussite à surmonter les souffrances rencontrées durant cette période de transition. Les initiés exhibent fièrement ces objets, offerts par leur mère ou un autre membre de la famille.

Bei ihrer Rückkehr nach der Abgeschiedenheit im Initiationslager erhalten männliche und weibliche Initianden oftmals Süßigkeiten und Geschenke, wie Schmuck und Uhren, die sie für ihr erfolgreiches Ertragen der Entbehrungen während der Übergangszeit belohnen. Die Initianden führen diese Artikel, die meist von Müttern oder anderen Familienmitgliedern überreicht werden, mit großem Stolz vor.

The desire to preserve indigenous traditions and customs of dress is still widespread, and even small children wear beads on festive occasions. Some beadwork necklaces and fringed aprons are made specifically for children, usually by their mothers. But, because they also wear long strings of beads and other items made for adults, children may look quaintly over-dressed.

Le désir de préserver les traditions autochtones et les coutumes vestimentaires est toujours très répandu; même les petits enfants portent des perles pour les occasions spéciales. Certains colliers et tabliers frangés sont fait spécialement pour eux, souvent par la mère. Cependant, comme ils portent aussi les longs colliers de perles et autres ornements pour adultes, ils paraissent souvent trop habillés et cocasses.

Das Bedürfnis, Überlieferungen und Brauchtum bei der Kleidung zu erhalten, ist noch weit verbreitet, und zu festlichen Anlässen tragen selbst kleine Kinder Perlenschmuck. Manche Ketten und Schurze werden besonders für Kinder angefertigt, gewöhnlich von deren Müttern. Da die Kinder aber auch lange Ketten und Zubehör tragen, das für Erwachsene angefertigt wurde, wirken sie oft drollig verkleidet.

The use of plastic beads has become increasingly common throughout South Africa. This has led to the production of unusually boldly patterned beadwork items and the introduction of colour combinations quite unlike those found on more traditional pieces.

L'usage de perles en plastique est devenu de plus en plus courant en Afrique du Sud. Ceci donna l'occasion de créer des motifs inédits et d'obtenir des nouvelles combinaisons de couleurs ne ressemblant guère aux styles des pièces traditionnelles.

Die Verwendung von Plastikperlen nimmt allerorts in Südafrika zu. Dies hat zur Anfertigung von Perlenarbeiten mit ungewohnt lauten Mustern geführt, und auch die Farbkombinationen unterscheiden sich gänzlich von denen der traditionellen Stücke.

The growing acceptance and use of plastic beads is partly due to the fact that it is quicker to produce beadwork garments with larger beads. Other factors, such as the high cost of smaller, glass beads, also account for this development, and for the use of different accessories like safety pins as decoration. In most communities, plastic beads are combined with older beadwork items.

L'utilisation croissante des grosses perles en plastique est due à la rapidité avec laquelle on peut maintenant fabriquer les diverses pièces. Il faut aussi tenir compte du coût plus élevé des petites perles de verre, et l'usage d'accessoires comme les épingles de sûreté, pour comprendre ce développement. Dans la plupart des communautés, on incorpore les perles en plastique dans les ornements plus anciens.

Die wachsende Bereitschaft, auch Plastikperlen zu akzeptieren und zu verwenden, ist teilweise darauf zurückzuführen, daß aus großen Perlen schneller Kleidungsstücke angefertigt werden können, aber auch auf andere Faktoren, wie Kostspieligkeit der Glasperlen und Verwendung neuzeitlicher, dekorativer Ergänzungen wie Sicherheitsnadeln. Oftmals werden Plastikperlen mit älteren Perlenarbeiten kombiniert.

It is common today to combine traditional clothing and beadwork with accessories made for other purposes. Christmas decorations, plastic trinkets and even newspapers add dramatic accents to the wearer's dress, including sparkling colour.

Il est commun de nos jours de voir des costumes traditionnels incorporant des accessoires modernes et imprévus. Des décorations de Noël, des babioles en plastique, des vieux journaux même, produisent un aspect frappant et renforcent l'effet des couleurs.

Es ist heutzutage üblich, traditionelle Kleidung und Perlenarbeiten mit Dingen zu kombinieren, die eigentlich für andere Zwecke hergestellt wurden. Weihnachtsschmuck, billiger Plastikschmuck und sogar Zeitungen werden mit dramatischem Effekt bei der Bekleidung verwandt. Auch ein verstärktes Gefühl für leuchtende Farben gehört dazu.

At their coming-out ceremonies, male South Sotho initiates wear sunglasses as a sign of deference and worldliness. Female initiates often carry ribbons with artificial flowers, probably in emulation of the accessories carried by modern-day brides.

A la fin des cérémonies d'initiations, les garçons south sothos portent des lunettes noires pour marquer leur importance. Les filles portent souvent des rubans et des fleurs artificielles, sans doute en imitation des accessoires portés par les jeunes mariées.

Bei der Einführungszeremonie tragen männliche Initianden der Süd-Sotho Sonnenbrillen als Zeichen des Respekts, aber auch der Weltgewandtheit. Weibliche Initianden tragen oft Bänder mit Kunstblumen, wohl in Anlehnung des Zubehörs einer modernen Braut.

The Swazi practice of fashioning decorations from wool can be compared to the use of plastic beads, in that items made from these materials do not require long hours of labour. During the 19th century in the reign of the third Zulu king, Mpande, members of the royal family and the king's warriors wore accessories made from wool obtained from the traders at Port Natal, later Durban.

La pratique swazie de façonner des ornements en laine remonte au 19ième; étant donné la rapidité de fabrication, elle peut être comparée à l'usage des perles en plastique. Durant le règne de Mpande, le troisième roi des Zoulous, ses guerriers et les membres de la famille royale portaient des accessoires confectionnés en laine obtenue des marchands de Port Natal.

Der Brauch der Swasi, Dekorationen aus Wolle herzustellen, könnte mit der Verwendung von Plastikperlen verglichen werden, da die Anfertigung der Artikel dann keine lange Arbeitszeit erfordert, aber der Ursprung liegt im 19. Jahrhundert. In der Regierungszeit des dritten Zulukönigs, Mpande, trugen Mitglieder der königlichen Familie und seine Krieger modisches Zubehör aus Wolle, die sie von den Händlern in Port Natal (dem späteren Durban) erwarben.

Young Zulu women wear beaded girdles on festive occasions like the Reed Ceremony and Shaka Day. The practice of adding studs dates to the 19th century when brass obtained from white traders were used. Today the studs are made from cheap alloys.

Les jeunes zouloues portent des ceintures perlées pour les occasions festives, comme la cérémonie des roseaux ou encore la fête de Chaka. La vogue d'insérer des clous date du 19ième, quand on pouvait obtenir du cuivre des marchands blancs.

Zu festlichen Anlässen wie dem Shaka-Tag tragen junge Zulufrauen Perlengürtel. Die Beifügung von Nieten datiert aus dem 19. Jahrhundert, als man von weißen Händlern Messing erwerben konnte. Heute sind die Nieten aus billigen Legierungen.